DIVERSION

Also by George Murray

Poems
Carousel
The Cottage Builder's Letter
The Hunter
The Rush to Here
Whiteout

Aphorisms
Glimpse

For children
Wow Wow and Haw Haw

DIVERSION

POEMS

GEORGE MURRAY

ECW PRESS

#CivilDisconvenience

What if Revelations had been called Revolutions?

Hang on a second while I google this.

Jesus laughed.

Fire breaks through the smoke the way sun breaks through the fog.

Quiet as an option silently dies.

Unforgettable facts wedge themselves like stains between our
       bedsheets.

Prayer's tinny voice squawks from an analog phone.

Most rioters eventually get distracted by mirrors.

I'd take *the calm before the storm* if it meant having any calm
       whatsofuckingever.

There are levels of speechless we haven't yet discovered.

Wanking is the other white meat of art.

The forecast follows the fearcast.

Horror becomes the state one occupies when seeing oneself quoted
       in the news.

Marginalia declared autonomy and formed a state.

People in the suburbs suffer from Stock Home Syndrome.

Who dares enjoy themselves anymore?

Remember to thank Christ you don't have to get off your couch.

Saying things gets only saying done.

Flames paint outer walls red the way televisions paint inner
       walls blue.

Down-the-way is where news happens.

Pluck the bricks flying by to rebuild your house.

Listen for the constant exposition of a man sure he's nailing a date.

We have the right to demand boredom.

Lassie keeps barking about how much Timmy likes it down the well.

Sadness retains its title as anger's most widespread illusion.

It's become apparent your fantasies just aren't interesting enough.

Civil unrest always evolves into parties.

Police hunch over coffee with their heads bowed and gun
            hands twitching.

Rows of driveways straight as bars on windows.

A Streetcar Named Covet.

I just realized my dick and head both loll the same way when tired.

Dollarama looted but the bookstore left untouched.

Staff the barricades!

We used to say *don't go into the woods* whereas now we say *don't read
            the comments.*

Cave wall shadows only work if there's a fire.

It appears that *decimate* now means to reduce by a factor of *holy fuck.*

Can anyone tell whether it's kindness or malice that's reached
            homeopathic levels?

Allow me to apologize in advance for my humanity.

Type that line as though something depended on it.

Your door rattles in the jamb but the lock is sturdy and continues to hold.

The armchair uprising has begun.

#ClockworkOrRage

Come all you haters and see what I have wrought.

Our primary role as teachers is to demonstrate how to best
waste time.

I survived Seamus Heaney and all I got was this lousy career.

Monuments are built daily to distraction.

The terms *rescuers* and *salvagers* are mostly interchangeable.

Before the sun has risen it is just a bright hill.

Only 24 men have walked on the moon and/or behind Jesus.

Crack the spine of *The Gutenberg Bubble*.

Statistically speaking there has to be a secret door around
here somewhere.

Moses flicked his cigarette into the dead bush.

Plan your strategic withdrawal from wishing everyone a happy
fucking birthday.

You have 73 important updates waiting.

A more likely zombie apocalypse would be a horde of abandoned
buildings.

What we call the sociopaths among us is *neighbours*.

The number of Aboriginal women missing from this line is difficult
to estimate.

Heaven don't want him and Hell's afraid he'll go Columbine.

Poets are the unacknowledged escalators of the world.

We all see dead people now.

The subtitles have been subtly lying to us for years.

Sleeper cells awaken and begin plotting in your spreadsheets.

Ennui is an alert that pops up to tell you there are currently
     no alerts.

The Illuminati left their lights on again.

Bombs strapped to our babies in their dear little TNT onesies.

A Room of One's Pwn.

If I had it to do all over again it would be a cookbook.

Simply breathing is moving forward.

Every breast exposed in the Sistine Chapel is a new big bang.

xx is right next to *cc*.

The emperor of YKK pulls himself together.

Look into the dead shark eyes of our leader.

You are what you contract.

Violence has an exchange rate against the price of oil.

I heard about him but I never dreamed he'd have blue eyes and blue jeans.

Truly elegant equations deserve cartouches.

Naked old men in flip-flops roam the change room with their
     hanging tits and balls.

Religion is like sucking in your gut while standing on the scale.

Glitter arcs from the TV remote.

There's been a sudden spike in the number of lives ended on knees in
     front of a SWAT unit.

I want to die with my boots on or at least my slippers.

Hitler's ghost slow claps in the silence men call Hell.

#DaydreamBereaver

You won't believe what happens next.

All money eventually finds its way to buying airtime.

Blisters on the roof of your mouth from either fried eggs or
    something you said.

The sliding scale of fuckable has no handrail.

Best not look at the parts per million.

December asteroid with a bull's eye almost hit by a passing planet.

Is it too much to ask you to act like porn said you would?

Bettie Page looks like a drawing of Bettie Page.

12,000,000,000 solar mass black hole sucks a golf ball through
    a garden hose.

Some proofs lead to surprising hypotheses.

It's increasingly difficult to find an uncrumbled wall to deface.

All the aneurysms you haven't had are gathered at their drawing board.

Every institution a movie set for a super-villain hideout.

The 12-year-old boys drift in the blue-smoke wind.

Brigitte Bardot is a poem I'd like to fuck.

Snowplows moonlight at mass graves.

A child raised in the refugee camp can't sleep in a house where
    the roof doesn't flap.

I wanted to tell you something neither of us knew.

Space is a gauge in the ear of God.

Now that Everybody-Gets-a-Trophy Day is over we can get down
    to business.

The world is too full of almost-good folks.

Beat your way past the flailing critical fists with your face.

Like a folder full of how-to videos saved for after the world's end.

#12 really blew my mind.

If George Lazenby's mole can survive being on George Lazenby then
you can too.

Shiny happy people stabbing backs.

What stale hell is this?

Lowercase letters wake for their midnight feeding.

I only need one more online IQ test to fuck Stephen Hawking over
for good.

Each city fumes like a bong's smoke chamber.

The matter/antimatter problem was the original mutually assured
destruction.

Homecoming queen becomes homestaying queen.

Disciples follow the guide with the umbrella and megaphone.

One flew over the cuckoo's nest but the rest of us landed in it.

Death switched to a pistol after complaints a scythe wasn't
individual-enough attention.

I like big buts and I cannot lie.

Freedom is the space found after the last channel on the dial.

The sound of our culture is the sound of a fat ass flopping onto
a toilet seat.

12 reasons you need to try this before you die! are 11 more than
needed to convince me.

What you're reading is a black box.

Bet you a dozen beers the first intelligent thought was a wish.

#UseYourEmojination

A house multiplied also cannot stand.

Disrobe consecutive olive pits with your tongue.

I'll even snip the plastic beer can rings if it means a break from
     hating myself.

Frankenstein's masterpiece missed his appointment to have his
     stitches removed.

Human is the state being occupies before learning to choose.

Busybodies wear looks on their faces to turn milk.

Cameraman straddles his cobra dolly and rises to get the right shot.

Think of all the mathematics inside the eraser.

MC1R is all up in my evolutionary grill.

You think I just fell off the back of a truck when really what I fell off
     was the wagon.

Dawn breaks like a mouth full of teeth.

Worry is the product of trying to fit infinite love into finite time.

Apocryphal selfies roam the borders of the profile's canon.

Remember to rhyme *mom* with *atom bomb*.

So much depended on that red wheelbarrow because it was used to
     transport the bodies.

This is where the blubber meets the road.

What if what was sewn together was ideas?

Anxiety is less like a ball in your stomach and more like a cube in
     your heart.

My two favourite words are *message* and *deleted*.

Bar chart of your stats forms the cliff from which you fling yourself.

The opposition still rushes you even though they say it's a level
    playing field.

Indifference is like water to me.

What we really needed was an army of Doris Lessings.

The blue plate special is the *Smurf 'n' Turf.*

Become the monster that aggregates all the channels.

Every book shaves a hair from my life like every prayer steals a piece
    of the preacher.

Wreckage-sifting is all the rage.

The fossil record will remember my milk carton before it
    remembers me.

Every time I sit still I increase my speed.

Poison is such a personal thing for both the one dying and the one
    making dinner.

You said *exercising* and I heard *exorcising.*

If you search far and wide enough you'll eventually find the bolts in
    the internet's neck.

This beheading brought to you by the letter *chop* and the number
    sword.

Enemies leave their laundry in your vestibule.

Lenses widen to get the whole moment but only spread to their
    point of view.

An incognito drunk scrambles to remain so.

Tesla coil tested with the sweat on the back of your balls.

Cities are retaken one at a time in the ways steps are by a stoner.

Maybe this is a good place to put a prayer.

Undead is just a word we invented to give more levels to the idea
of *alive*.

Narcissistic men will interrupt anybo—

#EasterEggStacy

There must be a billion funerals a day in Mario Land.

52-hertz whale picks up an old KGB numbers station in its teeth.

Celebrity is a commander at attention before an audience of soldiers
     at ease.

Were Madonna's arms always so veiny when miming something racy?

Porn is becoming its own countryside.

You see yourself as a perfect snowflake but you're part of a blizzard.

Look around the cave and count those who could murder.

Zombies the world over suffer from a Jesus-based inferiority complex.

Please wipe down the joystick after use.

Being makes the darkness light and the light start to throw shadows.

That storm front arrives like a boss.

Are you also being held hostage at any given moment by the number
     of men you have left?

Both God's and Nietzsche's emails are fatally undeliverable.

Stephen King has possessed the body of a ferocious Stephen King.

Every action is another quest for bliss.

Vote for this book in whatever contest is currently on your screen.

Schrödinger's cat is in its Xbox.

I'm getting firearms certified to defend my piece of the End Times.

Age makes the parts that should bend stiffen and the parts that
     should be stiff bend.

Guess the number of tsunamis in the jar and win!

Follow the teachings of the Lord on Twitter.

What do you call a town that even the ghosts have left?

Signatures are now alms.

It's easy to suspect everything worthwhile is fake.

Self-imposed diet restrictions are the new righteous piety.

CDC warns of a possibly unchecked spread of meanness through
    the population.

The water Jesus walked on wasn't even choked with plastic islands.

Ecstasy remains as mutable as it is momentary.

I can't wait to fill out the universe's customer satisfaction survey.

Sad soldiers are totally in these days.

Apocalypse makes the planet's hot parts freeze over and frozen parts
    carve ice hotels.

It takes 10,000 fans or one good murder to constitute fame.

Lying awake is the burden of intelligence.

Even the jay on the windowsill wants in.

Pac-Man and Master Chief fold around nothing as their death
    sounds wind down.

In the ocean's darkness there is a grinding.

The insides of some men are the colour of a switched-off screen.

Iron gates wrought to keep the riffraff out of our humanity.

Anger fades into itself like Kevin Bacon's jawline recedes into his neck.

Rocks roll back to reveal the world's empty caves.

All these cameras and yet still the children go missing.

#MarginalPersonalityOrder

Starlings vomit song and call it nature.

Hollywood is rebooting its World History franchise to interest
    new audiences.

Lanced thought bubbles suppurate white space.

Starving children would eat Ebola if it came in noodle form.

Pockets as choked with clacking billiard balls as a porn star's mouth.

The traffic lights glow like new scabs.

Starlets keep longer in the oven than freezer.

That's as fucked up and perfect as Freddie Mercury's overbite.

Magnetic poles speak magnetic Polish.

Hug that galaxy with open arms.

Chubby legs on a baby are the world's last honest pleasure.

That man with the plastic glasses never stops humming "Sonny's
    Dream."

Death is forever in the process of dying but never dies.

Politicians endorse the stupid fucking children.

Drunks stagger by in perfect stockings.

Always meet your mother in a public place far from home.

Clouds press down like a hand over your mouth.

Police are parked outside the neighbour's house but not doing
    anything.

Every stone is a fossil of something.

Those who don't listen closely are best shunned like a colony
    of leopards.

Blue chalk dust hangs like a breath before something long unsaid.

Hurricanes swirl in the satellite photo like nature's bleached
assholes.

It's hard to choose between the best popes.

Hungry people are more dangerous than starving people.

Spread flesh on the sheets like almond butter on bread.

Hunting for porn is now a kind of porn.

The next trick is getting all this AstroTurf to photosynthesize.

Accidental nakedness found in a gust of wind.

Time is a trellis on space's wall.

Professors keep fucking their students and teaching them lessons.

Narcissism is the DSM's Occam's razor.

Every word out of a royal's mouth shoots like spermless semen on the
world's face.

Boys fear women who refuse to fear men.

Practice first guessing first and second second.

The baby is almost as big as his Rambo knife now.

Sharpie on the stall door has lost its prophetic cred.

Don't pot the black ball just yet.

Announcements over the prison PA ping off suburban homes.

Neither smoking nor assfucking without a preparatory enema are
acceptable anymore.

Rifle envy is slightly less creepy than handgun envy.

Diagnose *this* motherfucker.

#OutLiars

It is time to shit in the houses of our dearest friends.

Listening to a child coughing in bed is virtually anxiety-free for me.

Pigeons anoint our monuments with reality.

To-do lists fall over you like shovelfuls of gravedirt.

Given it was a telephone wire you sat on I can't figure out how it is
your pants caught fire.

Our ears crackle as societal pressure changes.

Research all the surprising places the clitoris ends up going.

Origami cranes flock to the watering hole to find only ink.

The solar system is a Venn diagram of decreasingly unrelated ideas.

I bought my soul back from the pawn shop for twice what it's worth.

Heaven and Hell stake out opposite ends of the living room and stare
each other down.

Imagine the throbbing anger that is the Hulk's cock.

Rogue currencies exchange significant glances.

Oulipo is poetry's BDSM.

My cappuccino foam looks like an ass crack I'd like to fuck.

The farmer comes in from the field and wipes the bitcoin from
his hands.

Bracketed counters beside folder icons tick up faster.

Look at all the loose feet in this massacre photo.

I insist that this in fact *is* formal.

BabyGap is clothes made by babies for richer babies.

Tremolo wisdom warbles from a dozing pothead.

Volume control is a future civil rights issue.

Stick your finger up Saturn's rings and let's call ourselves hitched.

Taxis pull up to the crashed planes to wait for fares.

Run away with me from the tumbling buildings.

Who else was stoned to death today?

I hope God is happy now.

Give blood every six weeks whether or not you can find a clinic.

Every idea taken from below like a seal by a killer whale or a reverse
cowboy.

Austerity is what's *Owed on a Grecian Earn*.

Blinking first is what liars do last.

My sons will never know a world without a mute button.

Flinch at the thought of a ~~poetry reading~~ broken dick.

That rollercoaster-dip feeling of a plane in turbulence is now an
everywhere feeling.

Death's no biggie.

2.718281828459045235360287471352662497757247093699959574966967

Floor to ceiling windows look out onto the tops of your cheeks.

Latest crack smoking video is actually of a fissure leading straight
to Hell.

Truth's unit of measure is the telomere.

Forget poetry and just enjoy the unbridled collecting and hoarding of
every last thing.

There'll be time enough for the important stuff when I'm dead.

#UCan'tDoucheThis

Let's burn this fucking planet to the ground.

Mood is a disease.

There's a dumpster parked in the Anglican cemetery.

At the centre of the question lives the Minotaur with his axe
and raised eyebrow.

Everyone's still looking at us white guys but it just doesn't feel the same.

Sharpen the planks of your placards into stakes.

Tiny distances don't just belong Zeno.

Someone keeps asking us to show him our tits.

This is not what I intended.

Death's character was the first one added to the book.

The answer to *Which cosmological structure are you?* is *All of them.*

Einstein's Cross gets worn around every neck.

Parachutes covered in a series of interconnected zippers.

An Ali punch thrown underwater would still knock you the fuck out.

Being is the wound and the body its scar.

Lineups at the McDonald's are 10 times those at the church.

Texts chirp in an effort to fuck your eyes.

As usual men continue to explain their ownership of you.

There's always the option to just draw the underwear on with
a Sharpie.

Polite conversation murmurs its Muzak.

The musk of men in a January elevator has no solution except the
building's destruction.

We are always walking the Planck.

The truth can only be explained in powers of 10.

Flowers on the bush of possibility are called news items.

Don't let your invented marginality become a fetish.

Rhythm originates in the sunglasses.

Immune systems line themselves up against all the wrong
    battlefronts.

The planned blood transfusion from a shark goes off without a hitch.

Vibrations rattle up the flagpole that is scale.

Retarded guys sometimes just want to chat.

The tiniest movements of the feet are now considered dance.

Vaccines could have outlived their purpose.

All your accusations fail because you don't know me.

I look into each of your eyes and am disgusted by the hatred
    and want reflected there.

Excised human heart flesh soaked in warm seawater will try to beat.

Feminist tears taste just as salty.

Space smells like the barbeque at a NASCAR tailgate party.

A goth tanning salon opens at midnight.

There's nothing left to be done except concentrate on the children.

If we could tunnel through history the answer would reveal itself
    every step of the way.

Alright stop with the Hammertime.

#HookLineAndSinkHer

The gunman would like a cup of water.

Deep in the autumn brush rests the rusted carcass of a '59 Galaxie hardtop.

Compared to the slasher-psycho the shooter-psycho is practically
using a napkin.

The choices today consist entirely of German opera.

What's the deadliest way to tell a daughter to be careful?

The Handmaid's Tail.

SWAT officers sit shoulder-to-shoulder on a picnic bench.

Valkyries have the hottest pigtails and helmets.

Today's soldiers are always surprised to find themselves shot.

Buddhists get horny on sugar highs.

Don't look in the water when seeking the sublime.

A carload of boys circles like bearings rolling in a bowl.

Drop in your line but not your pole.

We're talking a pansexual-polyamorous-post-gender-pronoun
level of confusion.

Hipster beards meet at night to discuss the coming apocalypso.

Everyday-terrorism of dirty looks.

Forest becomes park once the city rings it.

Drag the rivers and throw back any unsought bodies.

UPS truck jumps the curb in front of the birthing centre.

Who wants to cut tall poppies when you can mow them?

Nervous tap of a diamond solitaire on the table.

The massage therapist's rack rests against your head as she wrings
your neck.

Activists spend more time -ivisting than acting.

This poem was written FPS-style with the best DLC weapon.

Arnold Schoenberg arrives at the 14th floor.

The difference between you and your bank account is pretty technical.

Whether the universe is cyclical or eternal doesn't really matter one
flying fuck.

There's no silence like the silence of a date in mid-failure.

Whoever poured the sea this morning filled it to the brim.

Broken glasses see around corners.

Little tent cards placed over camping bullet casings.

No one can get their phone up quickly enough to selfie with the suspect.

A bride leans against a wall to rest.

The waves keep rolling and the posters go up.

News is always another girl missing.

Tell my son to be a man instead of one-of-the-men.

Get right up close to the pool of blood if you want to count the teeth.

Twelve tones say so much.

Somewhere deep inside you're still willing to wear a Han Solo costume.

A bell rings and the killers clock in and out while nodding sheepdog-
and-coyote hellos.

That strange object in the sky turned out to be

Cower ye fools before the clock's blank face.

A ballcapped Pepsi truck driver turns his head to watch a schoolgirl
    cross the road.

The chimes and pings blend into one another.

Nothing is a story until it has its own novelty lunchbox.

Sour is the flavour of rush hour traffic.

Abuse is very gentle with itself.

Slanted books on the shelf slide against each other and sigh as they
    take time to die.

Fat moles stand erect from the skin like a copse of stubby dildos.

Morning curb stomps the clouds.

An empty spot sits just left of the moon.

Telemarketers line up on a wire like crows.

Irises dilate at the shadow's terminator.

The Tragedy of Spamlet.

All the most useful religious symbols can also act as crosshairs.

Drop of blood on the toilet rim.

Red lights allow time to reflect on the state of being stopped.

It's inconceivable now that Joshua was a tree before it was an album.

This year's Peace Prize goes to afternoon naps.

Bass becomes the anticipation while treble stays the scream.

Fall leaves trapped against a curb swirl themselves into sentience.

There's a line of cabs balls-deep outside the penitentiary.

Some days the news settles on the eye's skin like liquid nitrogen.

Face tattoos keep the grimaces dancing.

Death will come to all by serrated maple leaf.

People get loved despite being people.

Waiting was invented by those seeking sciences that explain the soul.

The still from a cinematic car chase looks like a parked car.

Caps lock is its own language.

Other worlds are too close to reach for.

Skin dies and dies and dies and keeps on being skin.

As surprising as a drunk with minty breath.

Why does the ladder need to stop when the building does?

Morning gets teabagged by event.

Without penmanship classes how will we write HELP in lipstick on
a car window?

October sun spreads its legs.

Licking the rust from exposed rebar will not solve the structural
integrity problem.

Friends have moments akin to bad poems in otherwise great books.

Time will always be a hair past a freckle.

Forsooth and fuck this newsfeed.

You look highest def in the reflection of a dead screen.

The caller pauses before hanging up.

#AdamAndExe

She pulls down the iPhone from the branch and bites.

Go forth and add!

You've sat so long on folded hands that the chair's wood has grown
up around you.

Ideas and spiked nog can both go off between concept and
consumption.

Think about how quaint IEDs now seem.

As stunned as a squirrel that's fallen out of a tree.

Why has it been so long since you thought casually about fucking
Jennifer Aniston?

Jealousy rolls around like a paraplegic cock that wants to be stiff.

The recipe ends with an instruction to cross-medicate to taste.

Failure is the milk that feeds the great.

Please state your case in both official genders.

The rose and weed both peer through the same fence.

Knowledge and bad decisions go together like Coke and a simile.

Fear hangs suspended in the rum like cherries in a cake.

Every moment of rest is a miracle performed by no one.

Once you realize you're in the horror film it's best to no longer
turn around.

Are you sure you want to delete this file?

Dreams line up like a playlist waiting to be viewed.

The faux jewellery box of a seabird's stomach.

Phone cord coiled around the finger like the serpent around a branch.

Life and death are separated only by rules.

Red notification flags pop up around each moment.

While awareness lasts I should probably ask whether I'll be able to
   come back from this.

Incidental islands form around our indulgences.

Eden just went public domain.

Brand protection gets its own military force and drones.

Ys pile up in the blood of our women.

Two in the bush leaves little room for anyone else.

You have to admit this is at least as entertaining as a domestic
   dispute two gardens down.

Let me know when you're quite finished handing out the names.

Public laughing is a contact sport.

Apps hang around like programs with ironic beards.

I'd like to teach the world to sing in perfect pharmacy.

The scrotum's puckered little brain sucks up tight.

Diverge and conquer!

We are cobblestones under thought's tourist carriage.

Stents are set to reinforce our tunnel vision.

Was it the selfies that tipped us off to the fact that we were naked?

I wish God would stop jerking us around.

The golden ladder let down from Heaven wasn't long enough to
   reach the ground.

Maybe I'll live longer if I stop ignoring the nonsense.

#TheKnownUniVersace

Love flattens time.

The groceries in the trunk hyperventilate beneath the locks.

Old men substitute video games for bathing.

It's a vegetarian act to eat a carnivore.

The sum of the squares of the first seven primes is 666.

Practising disdain now constitutes 60 percent of billable hours.

Dice rattle in the breath as though the chest were a craps table and
    each lung a cup.

The convention centre is also a mortuary.

I owe my soul to the company whore.

A fat man jogs in time lapse.

More effort goes into social media strategy than elevators.

Chinese knives lose their handles before the blades dull.

A thyroid lies naked in a dish.

The copyright text on sea salt flakes reads *Calvin Klein*.

Headaches keep a state of affairs more current than peace.

All the best meteors fall on Russia.

Heavy scent of makeup powder and cigarettes.

There are people who like to get liquored up before they go out to
    get liquored up.

Mirrors are a form of time travel.

An angel fakes a broken wing to draw predators away from its nest.

University degrees are chosen like earrings.

Your morals stepped out for a smoke and fell down drunk.

Red pants don't give a fuck.

Even the Vikings are zipping up.

It's lazy to seek converts when there are disciples to be had.

God is not yet Santa.

All the aprons and skillets and church bells are spattered with
liquid rust.

Sometimes the only way to mask crossing yourself is in a nose wipe.

The Collected Dicks of Emily Poeminson.

Supermassive black holes draw in and push out like cunts in the night.

Gabriel's Horn is hatted by math.

There's no more room in the basket for heads.

Only at the end of the day does one notice one's glasses were filthy.

Cosmological structures know all about real estate.

We need more boots on the ground zero.

Freebases loaded and four out.

Gravity dines at the table of you.

That line drawn in the sand turned out to be stolen from Jack Benny.

A doorknob sits under a sewer grate as though thankful to catch
a small break.

The sequel you wrote to Revelations is still out with your agent.

Don't forget to erase the slate.

#HeroesAreMadeNotBourne

You win you loser.

A year without an end-of-the-world date is like a year without
Christmas.

Worth is now measured in loyalty card points.

Once we get bored with being naked under the skin is the only place
left to go.

The porn channels are endless and yet never enough.

I'll believe in God once the autistic people do.

The can of whup-ass I opened turned out to be Italian Wedding soup.

Your firmware is showing.

The bricklayer skips the clay and cements together a wall of leather
wallets instead.

All the treasure drops increase.

You sat on the can so long you forgot whether you already shat.

Who will you hide behind in the last days?

Cops form a circle and whisper.

Too sick to be clean and yet not well enough to be dirty.

Children of gods and retards compete for airtime.

Hair is judged on its ability to withstand a good pull.

Like a bazooka mounted on a tricycle.

The Xray tech will scan you with her Sinéad O'Connor eyes.

Even the fetal alcohol kids have to go to school.

It's difficult to learn to touch when you were taught to push.

Angels and monsters are assembled in the same offshore sweatshop.

Clocks watch our hands in alarm.

Thinking floats on a sea of amusing videos.

One day perfume will help us hunt down the wicked.

You are the disease and I am the curation.

An emotionally significant ornament falls from the tree.

Dancing on the Céline.

The frequency of blessings granted increases with the decline
of religion.

Falling through the Earth only takes 42 minutes if all logic is ignored.

Old men now fancy themselves time insurgents.

Medusa was the original white rasta-girl.

Jesus stands to address the cast of *Seinfeld* at his Last Brunch.

Black rhinos fade out like obsolete programming languages.

The goal was Nerfed to poetic competence so everyone would feel good.

Who held the door open for you during the torrent?

Demand more from your riots.

Today someone photographed my brain as it commanded my muscles
to remain still.

Faster than a rolling bullet.

A world as promising as a ladder leaned against a dumpster.

The failures line up for another try.

Release the kraken.

#FaceYourFierce

Signal loss is a disappearing risk.

Clouds gather and ring like a crowd of faces looking down at a fallen man.

The meter maid is just happy to have a job.

Cigarette hanging from the mouth of a dude in overalls mowing a
government lawn.

Attach a brush to your mouse and see if your nothings make a painting.

What are the filthy secrets behind the voices on the radio?

Someone in this very crowd is looking at your face and imagining
spreading bruises.

All the videos play now whether you're there or not.

Everyone keeps parsing the everything of everyday.

The same future that was once dial tone became handshake then
silence then chime.

Emphatic gestures of a sleazy man talking to himself.

Shakespeare knew the worst of it.

Thirty seconds of quiz clicking confirms your metal is particle board.

He's trying to get her to his apartment and she's thinking of her
math homework.

Leaf blowers make the sound that best represents humanity's failure.

This is the latest video of someone doing something dangerous to
make me want to puke.

I am backwards compatible with life.

Nina Simone did this song but so much better.

Owed is the ocean bad men sail on.

Time's ghost wails around us.

. . . And that's when they discovered that life was a cosmic
    drive-thru line.

Schoolgirls swap horror stories like hockey cards.

Little lost laptop between Wi-Fis.

God and the Devil are a ratio and Man the slash between.

Meters tick away in the many backgrounds.

In the distance a pussy farts and someone claims it as their art.

There's dark and then there's amen dark.

What makes me free is I know the ability to trust will come back to me.

Clocks on the floor click slower than those on the walls.

We must record and quote back to each other the snarls of monsters.

Lines do not connect points so much as house them.

Baby's first cry is his log-in and first thought his password.

You see *memes* where I see *me-mes*.

Celebrity will one day be seen as a form of indecency.

As remarkable as a butch in cherry pumps.

Peace may be one of those concepts that never actually existed as
    a thing.

All that covers the dynamite in a terrorist's vest is a Volta.

If she's old enough to talk it's likely she already knows.

The original crowdsourcing was revolution.

And yet the sun keeps coming up as though the pressure is changing
    beyond the horizon.

No means no one said you could speak.

#UndisclosedIncipients

Expect delays.

The shredder whirs away somewhere under its paper mountain.

Boys with fresh faces and worn minds line the streets.

Keep God out of the prayers.

Some cut scenes are just longer than others.

When princes quit their armies I start to worry about war.

Turn the page to take notes and find it already filled.

You never notice a woman checking out your finger until you have
        a ring on it.

Bruise on the ass the shape of a fist.

Cancel all therapy appointments on Mental Health Day.

The victims have been bled into silver cups.

Neck tattoos and a wet cough fall in love.

Breathe quietly into the sunrise of those who hate you.

One Christmas decoration managed to survive the year on
        top of a credenza.

Entire languages go quiet one at a time like a clichéd choral piece.

Which side of the marital bed is happiest?

The collective noun for a pile of spilled Xanax pills is a *stare*.

English is the thing that will be the thing.

You need to spend part of your life with a user to learn how not be used.

That dog *does* look like Putin.

Let's just make sure Bela Lugosi remains dead.

Vileness gets whispered over a cabaret table.

The jet stream whips overhead with its severed electric cable crackle.

Pile of pink slips deep enough to sleep in.

All the class and glare of a bare bulb hanging in the living room.

Everyone who waits runs the risk of finding out there's no after-credits scene.

Holiness grows proportionally to volume.

Prince's face hangs its Halloween mask from a hook on the back of a door.

Each klaxon blares its robotic *ouch*.

Unification is just knotting.

Leadership works best in pamphlet form.

The evening news is the world's equalizer and it is now maxed out on treble.

Glass syringes crushed back into a white beach.

It's a generational thing to have fucked more than three Beckys.

Cloud cover only protects shooters in the sky.

The wind continues to look for a flute.

A confetti rain of paper gets called pages when what's on them belongs together.

Let's hang disease map prints in the teens' rooms.

Jesus doesn't know everything you've been up to but he does have his suspicions.

Three unreturned calls is all the leeway you get.

My favourite weapon is my wife.

#SocialMedea

Kill your darlings quickly in case they are someone else's darlings.

Envy and inferiority are best dealt with through childishly parodic
Twitter accounts.

Who the fuck could possibly care?

Praying feels to me like fumbling with buttons on a shirt tailored
for women.

Tranströmer's robots in the skies.

What is up with the trash collectors leaving the crowds behind?

Think of the intimacy lost since we stopped cleaning each other
with our mouths.

Death is a sprinkled donut on a string just out of reach.

Your latest vague statement got me thinking about myself.

Horny fairies know love is true in fairy tails.

Remembering something is actually remembering the last time you
remembered it.

The stone lobbed into the group of soldiers sets them to firing on
each other.

Elvis is mainly a figurehead king now.

Sadness's whale needn't come up for air.

Even the rich and famous are still on the hook for blowjobs.

Children are signatures written in blood.

This goddamn jacket is only 10 percent George Clooney.

Everyone wants a salacious piece of anguish's latest triumph.

If I only could have held Wisława Szymborska before she died.

All the explodable monuments stand on chairs and hike their skirts.

The time on her face is six minutes to midnight.

Critics are now mostly valves and drains.

It is a time best suited to the voices of mental cases.

A net is just thousands of bridges with no land between.

I'd tap that to the beat of "Wipeout."

Clickbait preceded clicking.

Satan sidelines as the Tooth Fairy for monsters.

Worship pulses its sonar ping into the mind's empty ocean.

One Hundred Years of Solitaire.

I want you all to have as many lols as you can fit in your margins.

The firefight sounds like a string of mistimed firecrackers.

It's almost lunch so please keep posting those hilarious baby Polaroids.

Untrained soldiers are called *people.*

No parking except by permit.

Intelligence *is* artificial.

All men could be kings if they pissed off the right witches.

City parks with their robot statues and fields of buried teeth and
    maybe-sleeping bodies.

Beware the I'ds of March.

Everyone is welcome to kneel down and watch.

In a minute or so I will probably think of something much more
    important.

The army withdraws and spills all over your stomach.

#TheBookOfExoduh

She made an ark of bullshits and set the child adrift.

Traffic lines up to flee every direction's apparent apocalypse.

Earth was hollowed out as though all the chocolate in Planet
     Neapolitan was underground.

The only inventive actions left involve a cock in the hand.

Each thought is the ghost of a tumour.

Assume now any candlelit faces you see are mid-vigil.

Take the *i* out of *je suis* and be saved!

Some shooters have a *cause* and some just have a *because*.

God wore Bermuda shorts to do His cannonball into the Red Sea.

Keep the eraser out of the pencil's reach.

What I like about the French is that they never really leave
     the barricades.

I may be slowly dying but at least I'm not fastly dying.

Stop thumbing through photos of skin diseases hoping for a match.

The gunmen disappear back into the crowd of gunless gunmen.

Defendant charged with inability to distinguish between 14
     and fuckable.

All the best heart attacks happen in the driveway.

Whenever I peer in pain and distress through a blizzard I think *Ben?*

Tsunamis are now in charge of all cartography.

Bestseller lists are weekly pantheons.

Now seems more than it was a moment ago.

Flower is a more beautiful verb than noun.

Bees fall silent to remind us what silence means.

Time is a dagger without pommel or tip.

Mushroom clouds are best served sautéed with fava beans and a nice Chianti.

Did the pitch break the bat or the hit?

Life is most rewardingly lived in a Cheerios commercial.

The motherfuckers shake with impotent rage instead of sticking to fucking mothers.

Smoke stack needs a light.

Bullies believe they are a form of currency.

Kalashnikov is the world's most important and influential brand.

The second hand unwinds while the first winds up.

Day moon like a crusted milk ring on a blue breakfast table.

All failure is *levitation failure*.

1.6180339887498948482045868343656381177203091798057628621354448

Blood used to paint a cave wall got the first Oscar for special effects.

The best you can ask is that the custody handoff goes smoothly.

We used to call folk wisdom *wisdom*.

Education wiggles its puppeteer's hand and your mouth moves accordingly.

Weathermen up their rhetoric in the face of terror in the news.

As Babylonian as a clock and as Protestant as time.

The real question is not whether He wrote it but which finger God actually used.

#HelterSkeletor

Hands are the original necklace.

We each keep mental lists of the heroes we've murdered.

Memo arrives with this week's instructions for anxiety typed in
    Comic Sans.

The floors rise up against us as we fall.

Black and white combined now make brown instead of grey.

You suspect your favourite game chirped important info when it
    knew you weren't there.

Keep switching channels faster in lieu of changing yourself.

Television's day as mankind's primary source of lighting draws to a close.

Remember that masks worn long enough become faces.

I ache to smash you out of existence.

You say Dumas and I say *dumb ass.*

Each witch's tit flashes its cold peek.

Soon the muscles will dispense with skin.

Things are looking up in the way people do when they've been
    knocked to the floor.

Catch the fallout on your tongue.

21 ways to keep your jail cell free of clutter.

Riots are just punk-assed revolts.

The latest piece of laboratory equipment is a ball gag.

Abdomens are the most common sheaths.

What we're ready to call *life* is spreading out.

Sometimes Charlie's angels are just the bugs crawling on Charlie's skin.

Flashing lights are like Heaven on Earth for the bored.

You could spend every moment of the rest of your life watching porn
    and never finish.

I would like a planetary topography smooth as the inside of a
    wedding band.

There will be someone who decides to hate this to rescue prosody.

Schoolgirls mill about in their pens.

Texts flutter in like confetti thrown from a convertible Cadillac.

AM radio keeps its own church.

Look to the ugliest among us for leadership when the world ends.

All is now like watching a stroke happen from inside your own
    he@D#$maS*Arj&dHijWz

This is becoming a good day for evil.

Your mother-of-pearl snap buttons are just waiting for you to fuck up.

Brains chew and spew information like black holes.

Eye sockets want to be bullet casings.

That sparkle in your son's eye is just the reflection of an LED.

In the future bondage gear will be formal wear.

Black is the barrel of a gun and white the flash within it.

Tell the children the only way to avoid capture is to stay small or
    grow too big for the cuffs.

All the books are already out at the prison library.

The sciences are killing our fetishes.

I have the power.

#BearingWitless

The children did not return before dark.

You may have to settle for a Sylvia Plath photograph if no Sylvia
moment comes.

It's harvest time at the server farms.

Twelve plus one is an anagram for *eleven plus two*.

Wineglass stems and bases look like spilling water and pools.

Barricades enjoy department store windows.

At the edge of the woods lovers hump in a dark car slowly filling
with CO.

Square roots triangulate beneath round bushes.

Comets have longer tails and bigger dicks than other harbingers.

If you connect the dots in the Oort cloud it reads *Do Not Disturb*.

The contents of the fruit bowl are a decaying data set in need
of analysis.

Some races break their ribbon at the starting line.

Faith is quicksand into which none know they're falling.

Marvel at the sheer Elvis-ishness of this moving knee.

The clever sign we crafted to hold up in this audience is sure to get
us on camera.

A Sale of Two Titties.

Laptop fan grill burn on the thighs.

Minds invent scenery to impress and explain the body.

I once stood in the Sistine Chapel and what I remember is I stood
once in the Sistine Chapel.

Wee Degas moments seem a little sketchy.

Luck carves its nature similar to time.

Power outages dare to split the middle of televised wars.

We will be in the future when we can watch reality TV set in
the distant past.

Police chief pulled over in a hoodie.

You'd be surprised how long a two percent battery can last.

Magic rings mingle in toolboxes with washers in baby food jars.

Space seems so empty and wrong without TIE fighters.

Occasionally I forget Libya exists.

Flipped-table-righter is an unpaid occupation known as love.

You're a Muppet but the hand up your back that moves your mouth
is your own.

"Amazing Grace" sung from the toilet.

Heaven's fire extinguisher is not WHMIS compliant.

Fireflies batter like kidnapped girls in a van's cargo bay.

One of the bodies has *x*'s for eyes while the other just reads *TILT*.

This Polaroid is taking forever to fade in.

Any song for children is creepy if you sing it while weeping.

Roaming charges creep up like a crooked stock ticker.

There'd come a point in the zombie outbreak when I'd just say *fuck it*.

My black sister and I both want to believe I'm listening.

I'd fuck the me I claim to be.

The shooter fled the scene in an unmarked car.

#BelieveEverythingYouHere

Every blank space is a comment box.

The purpose of event is to compete for spots on the evening news.

Chips of rust fall from the drones with frozen blue piss.

Everything happening is just a shim straightening the dangerous tilt
of a famous poem.

Fad diets line up for their turns.

Noon is not enough between sunrise and sunset.

A cold scrotum pulls itself up into something useful like cauliflower.

Nine of 10 ministers' wives are named Kathy.

The situation is so unfunny even Harvey Korman isn't laughing.

A giant ceramic needle set into the grooves of a blue whale's belly.

You see *legacy* and I hear *leg/assy*.

Women in hijabs also play badminton.

The delete button is all that will save us.

Old men don't fist bump so much as try to shake arthritic hands.

If Flaubert were alive today he'd be guesting on a Christina Aguilera
track as *Flo-Bert*.

Sleep is a time spent curled like Stephen Hawking.

Florists are the opposite of growers.

Saturn is only now returning to the spot where it was when you
were born.

Yet more inspirational Buddhist yoga advice breeds on Facebook.

There are not nearly enough side effects from what you've done.

Incense sticks ash-out on the graves of loved ones.

Control over what comes next will be what's lost next.

Use a hammer to anchor a stubborn screw.

Keep *cower* in reserve for the day *brash* fails itself.

Telegraphed punches mostly still get delivered.

Hank Williams would tell you the truth of it if he could.

The hymnal page numbers are all the same.

Hard-on ridges define themselves against checkered French
    underpants.

Flesh hangs in the darkest ocean and calls itself cetaceous.

Coffee shops are training grounds for teens learning to flash their
    panties at old men.

Fuck India and the rest of the world and rape.

There's only one pseudonym left for leaving anonymous comments.

Overhead the contrails are a map of unwritten Tweets.

Soldiers in the black and white wars still saw their blood in colour.

The woman will sit on your face when she's damn well ready.

Saying no like an involuntary Richard Pryor head.

Zero sense gets made in the factory of a day.

Tongues stuck in the battery terminal of gossip will catch on fire.

No one survived the series of events that eventually led to this
    perfect moment.

All the line breaks pulled from one book of poems equal a stammer.

Someone please send helicopters.

#SuicideBalmer

This season's explosive vests are by Betsey Johnson.

Whispers draw more attention than shouts.

Today's fiery crash doesn't have the same surprising zing as
    yesterday's.

Everyone checked CNN at once and the site collapsed under
    advertising manager cum.

Being is water circling a drain.

What they mean by non-perishable goods is goods that won't perish
    before you.

Pearls form around last words on the tongue.

Terza rima is a railroad track.

Passengers shuck off their mortal tattoos and go free.

Immerse yourself in the crackling poetry of the misheard drive-thru
    attendant.

Today the circus that kids run away to join is ISIS.

We understand enough to be worried but not enough to be terrified.

Each selfie a mugshot in the mind's booking room.

Who needs blinds when you can stack beer bottles in the windowsill?

Under the snow is vomit and under the vomit are syringes and under
    it all is the Earth.

Deformity rolls out into the genome like software patches.

It's all free for the first six months.

One day megastorms will seem as quaint as megabytes do now.

My anxiety is a large rodent in an onion skin bag.

God's small mercies are covered between news segments.

My very best happens when I start planning for planet-level
    disasters.

Anything stored in the cloud ends up looking like a castle.

I wuv you this much.

Sometimes I wish for the apocalypse just so I don't have to get dressed.

What about the contract signed in spit?

Conscious decision to not listen to that part of the mind that knows
    what needs to be done.

Small men look even smaller in Teamsters jackets.

Quadcopters haven't yet figured out how to weaponize their revolt.

There's one voice cackling out of sync in my head's laugh track.

People line up to board the latest Hindenburgs.

The economy is now evenly split between oil and penis enlargement.

Who is Vladimir Poutine?

It's quicker to skip the story and just take note of the death toll.

We're all looking for the wrong black box.

If exclusion were a currency the young would be printing money.

An imaginary testicle sprouts a real ingrown hair.

For a long while I just hid in one of Wystan Hugh's wrinkles.

Beside the photos of the wreckage is an ad for vacations in the
    country of the crash.

So many truths we can't see the facts.

The universe goes on whistling its mysterious Dixie.

No popcorn will be on offer in the final moments.

#AssAndYeShallReceive

Every day has become a Jesus Christ Shitshow Day.
Vaccine needles baptize themselves in the blood puddles beneath
    every child's skin.
Time and I have not been on speaking terms since forever.
Weekly Top 10 was cancelled because there's only nine songs now.
Bones clack in a duffel bag used for exchanging money.
Plant your feet and hold as though this mall hallway is the hill you've
    chosen to die on.
Noon is the bitching hour.
Parents frequent Sesame Street's seldom seen Red Light District.
Juvenile depth doesn't belong solely to the oeuvre of Rush.
The wasted words of a recently painted toilet stall.
Ephemeral selfie glimpsed in a mirror.
The laptop smells like fire when it runs cute cats and strenuous
    boredom porn.
Anonymous comments arrive one at a time like solipsistic anal beads.
My fists are rolls of gold quarters.
This is why classic rock is dying.
I'm left with my tongue up the ass of tomorrow and my cock in
    the mouth of yesterday.
The primary currency of this moment is distraction.
Old is what happens to nude when it continues to be itself.
I contain multiples.
FREE BIRD!
Each flashing moment an expired parking meter.

Give the finger at sunset in case the silhouette of our transiting
    planet is being observed.
The server statistics show spikes in unemployed bandwidth at 10 a.m.
Hope and despair have both been mathematically eliminated.
GIFs go round and round like syphilis.
Old men twist their eyes to ensure the girls don't catch them looking
    up their skirts.
This is a world dying of solutions for sale.
Everybody's last nerve is the plastic loop anchoring a price tag to a
    charity store sweater.
Political decisions release their little Armageddons.
Tread carefully here because I haven't yet salted this particular earth.
Gimme just one foul thing I don't already know.
This second has almost enough gravity to become spherical.
Phantom hip buzz is the new tinnitus.
Doesn't a Godhead imply the likelihood of a Godass?
Why don't news networks just use the live subtitles as the teleprompter?
Thy rod and staff comfort me and all the ladies.
Billboards are now just homeless TVs.
Spiritual singers climb the charts only to find "Stairway to Heaven"
    at the top.
Burlap sacks and twine belts mistakenly stored right next to the
    pitchforks and torches.
If I were black I hope I'd be doing more than this bullshit right here.
Don't forget to nod amen.

#TheGospelAccordingToLuck

Let he who is without stones cast the first stone.

The poem is over-written by the first word.

You're the only one who suspects there's been a miscommunication.

That lump in your throat just wiggled.

Somewhere below the bottom edge of the page is an open mouth
       pointed up.

All men are equal in the brotherhood of rape (Y/N circle one).

Narcissists never look in the same mirror twice.

Sleet assfucks the autumn and your plans both.

A chorus of angels sings ringtone jingles.

The dog turns both its nose and ass into the wind as though each
       senses its own thing.

Campfires create building lots in the night.

Japan bends its will on automating high magnitude quakes.

I never wanted to be the machine I became.

The evenings are your own failure.

Mothers close their wombs in strike.

The software that is Today has system requirements I am
       increasingly unable to meet.

Soon mental intolerance will be the fashionable excuse
       for everything.

Cowboys die of perpetual squint headaches long before
       the Marlboros get them.

A galaxy makes devouring its neighbour top priority.

The cleaned clock is full of copper and blood.

Night looks you up and down as though you were a demon on
      a Black Sabbath shirt.

Bad grammar is the jewellery of fools.

Hatred and lemonade are sold at roadside stands.

Treadmills pass away under us without fear or consequence.

Keep your feet moving to a BeeGees drumline.

The Devil drinks holy water with salt and lime before the spit take.

Gospel just wants to be a word again.

Old men still whisper their secrets even though the world gave up
      trying to hear.

Pills stay the same size while the dosage goes up.

Windows are a house's stanza breaks.

Remove the models and just leave what's been photoshopped.

The rib bones have formed a feminist collective.

Business cards melt in a wallet.

It was Elizabeth Bishop in the library with a candlestick.

The complicit never sit still in the same silence twice.

Shrug in and out of your own body like a shirt but wear hers like
      a gold ring.

Lean on the sash and shout down the snow.

That buzz in your pocket is a pop-up reminding you that today is
      Judgment Day.

Critics' loins are aflame right now!

Vader's "Imperial March" plays in my head whenever I approach
      a classroom.

We'll all get what's coming to me.

#AvengeMyBreath

In Xanadu did Newton-John a freaky pleather-dome decree.

Heaven fills up with dogs and lesser popes.

Cut in half a circle of fifths to make a chromatic rainbow.

Meteors tangent the planet and skip their cataclysms back into space.

Police say the victim and assailant were known to one another.

The genocide expert's accent is too thick to understand but there
        isn't time anyways.

Rome wasn't spilt in a day.

An ambulance sits outside the cathedral on Good Friday.

He speaks as though he has a pimple on his tongue.

Bird ghosts only walk.

Rock and roll is using a guitar pick to scratch your lottery tickets.

Gendarmes round up gendarme-costumed actors on a porno set.

Danish albums arrive in the mail again.

Hoodie strings hang like an idiot's garrote.

You have to take the sample mid-stream for this one.

Skin is a kind of armour.

All the news fit to print comes in flyer form now.

Splinters chip from every wooden eye.

A million lights dancing slightly out of sync is just called *light*.

Coronal mass ejaculation.

There's nostalgia in realizing that now is the only possibility.

A one-size-fits-all crown.

Murderers are one-person riots.

Tsks from a cranky old lady are the chick-chick-chicks of life's hi-hat.

Monks chant harmonies for girl choirs.

Santa's knowledge of your sleeping habits isn't creepy or legal.

The last good band name caused a brawl among dirty musicians.

Keep some confidence as your shield and make the rest your sword.

This is as sexy as 41 can be.

All the psychopaths start to bioluminesce.

The equator's tracksuit waistband cinches tighter.

Since the advent of robot handjobs in Japan we don't even need
ourselves anymore.

These kids today have solid selfie-esteem.

3.141592653589793238462643383279502884197169399375105820974944

I can't keep up with which aspects of my life I should be ashamed of.

Do miles fall just behind you or other directions as well?

The circle of life touches a line of inquiry.

Wipers push away the snow even as the motor burns out.

Aiming piss directly at shit stains on the porcelain is not
a public service.

This woman's pigeon-growling stomach just warbled a bar of
"Ave Maria."

Hey you with the sad eyes.

#DaysEndConfused

Today the country feels the way Terry Sawchuk's face looked.

English expanded until it broke like a condom.

The comments have been closed to prevent us further embarrassing
ourselves.

It's easy to want a woman who whistles.

One day you have a child and the next she's allowed to drive and fuck.

Someone searches only for compound fracture photographs.

Might I suggest the rack of iamb?

Satisfaction is scratching your back with a knife.

It's more honest to measure your speed relative to the galactic core.

Antiques sit under their polish and continue to rot.

Infinity plus negative infinity equals who the fuck cares?

Learn to speak our jargon or go back where you came from.

The web stats bring reality into sharp relief.

Cabbages conquer the flowerbed.

The small Portuguese man in tight jeans has as fine an ass as any
you've seen.

Headspin is a primary mode of transport.

We broke the weather but glued it back together with a tear-and-
denial paste.

It's raining unstable candy canes in all the best dreams.

The Laughterhouse Five.

Adulthood is the process of forgetting childhood.

I'd rather throw all I have in the trash than share even a single
piece with you.

Poland is way bigger than you remember.

Sidewalk mannequin in a parka but no pants.

Game the customs restrictions for fame and glory.

Your hand cream may be made from chemical explosives.

Screams have no accents.

Twenty years later and the screws and pins are still in there.

A standing ovation is now the expected minimum.

The zombie apocalypse has been in progress for 30,000 years.

Xray of a pot roast shows a brain inside.

Beckoning is a thing the undecided do.

Inflammatory critics are probably just gluten sensitive.

Getting dizzy from successive double takes.

The only thing worse than driving through Naples is stopping there.

Volume is becoming a synonym of meaning.

Tell Fritz to stop being a Deutschbag.

We go through this film as doomed as ladies or non-white men.

Borders are an old-fashioned programming language.

Unmarked vans are always marked by someone.

The air hangs painfully inside itself like a sore throat without any
        flesh around it.

Francophonely my dear I don't give a damn.

#ThePathOfLeastExistence

Gospel radio hangs still in the ear like boozy fat in the liver.

As machines with emotions go the universe isn't particularly evil.

Filth itself is the simplest medium.

Science rocks back and forth between conclusions like the neck of
       a happy fellator.

At least Reagan's end was a baggageless red button.

There's only one thing ruining our young men today and that is our
       old men.

I have always confused St. Peter and Colonel Sanders.

Photographs of flames don't tell the whole story of fire.

Faith is my axe handle and opinion my palm.

Charm and mercy are the open carry guns worn on our hips.

Your mom said you were as handsome as the Devil on
       a second date.

Everything darkens to William Faulkner's *Spanktuary*.

I miss the blue screen behind the *1-800 number* part of commercials.

The Circle of Life is a condom ring in a wallet.

An open line call-in show enumerates all the world's tiniest ills.

Piles of Percocet are swept with a push broom to the centre
       of the room.

Vanquished armies retreat leaving behind bodies and strappy heels.

Later evidence suggested murder-suicide in the video/radio
       star case.

Neither hologram nor reality theories are very appealing.

The day's minister stands before a peacock's tail of stained glass.

Don't get me started on the sirens.

Praying seems a bit like spinning a dial hoping to land on a station
worth listening to.

Eucharists fly like frisbees at the happy dogs of every mouth.

I can't remember whether Crystal Gayle was one of the original
Muppets.

The best thoughts open like gull-wing doors on a DeLorean.

Fat people really seem to love Birkenstocks.

1985 was just scary enough for girls to bargain away all their holes'
virginities with me.

Gentle Jesus gets his own gardening show.

Look in the mirror and know without doubt that nothing is looking
back at you.

James Joyce put the *art* in fart.

Sad facts have a way of becoming sad suspicions before they become
other sad facts.

The mayor's lip hangs its idiot's apostrophe.

Forgotten ideas collect above your head to form mood.

I can't remember the name of the knight who took minutes at
Arthur's Round Table.

Outcomes replace considering outcomes.

I suspect I have insomnia but am probably sleeping through it.

Worship regulates nervous breakdowns.

Anonymous comments overtake fists as the prime communicator
of misogyny.

There are only a few more words to read and they are so very much
     like a wafer-thin mint.
Besides how it all happens there's also how a man will explain it to you.
Allow me to offer you a towel for under your knees.

#AdmissionOfGilt

Prime can have 2 or 3 or 5 or 7 or more definitions.

I've started a petition to ask myself to please stop letting black
      people die.

Photos are now designed to be cried over.

Autumn is a billion branch assholes finally releasing a billion
      dangling leaf shits.

Cat poems are where I draw the line.

The strobe light of my disbelief keeps winking.

Droids not drones!

We don't die so much as dissolve into mathematics.

Your head is a barrel of monkeys and your brain a set of collars.

Books degrade more than biodegrade.

This morning's outrage is superseded by this afternoon's.

I've started a petition to ask myself to please stop treating women
      like shit.

We are all minions.

Prime numbers are like the girls you could never bed.

Robots will find those who ran them through their endurance tests.

Facebook photo albums are the new illustrated manuscripts.

The cake is a half-truth.

Basquiat's baby talk in a cage match with Schiele's hookers.

Melt dollar bills and use the goo to paint that body lying
      on the bed.

I've started a petition to ask myself to please stop pigging out
      in front of the poor.

Measurement's joke continues to be played on us.

It's all so free that it's all not enough.

My bank's CEO could rent my back as a coffee table.

Surely there's a billionaire out there who has all Batman's stuff but
can't be bothered.

The concept of us has already reached an age the reality of us will not.

Someday my prints will come.

The inability to fit into a pattern is a pattern.

Ragged fingertips where strings made callouses and laziness let
them fade.

Bears move in next door with their leather and Ikea furniture and
garbage tipping.

Primes are like carbon in the math's ecology.

I've started a petition to ask myself to please stop flicking matches in
the planet's tinder.

My exchange rate is overinflated.

How long before you consider tearing out pages for food?

I fancy my ashen face camouflage for the coming age of whiteouts.

Let the news wash over you like molten gold.

Idolize any moment of doubt.

Your skull keeps your brain from rolling apart like a halved cabbage.

I've started a petition to ask myself to please stop medicating my
boredom with violence.

God how I wish there was a lesser relative I could lose to terrorism.

The story continues before rather than beyond the book.

When the question is *Who's killing who?* there's no doubt the answer
is *It's us killing you.*

#WorthThePriceOfEmission

The only thing left to deal with is our addiction to being killed by monsters.

What was all the hating over?

Christmas sneaks up like a rusty train.

Sit still and see if you can feel your cerebrospinal fluid pulsing.

Thoughts get in deep like drains and infections.

Sky isn't just air anymore.

What if you die before the next *Star Wars* comes out?

Slush crunches like knuckles on day six.

Children imagine that at night their toys come to death and have
       tea parties.

We cling to our most useless things like grudges.

Solar powered forgetfulness.

Our habits are dollar stores that sell us our own plastic shit.

What if sickness is the only homunculus?

A tether runs from each free man to the satellite watching him.

Vaccines hang in their ampoules and dream of escape.

If there's one lesson life has taught us all it's to not don't be a rock star.

Leaf through *The Divine Sitcomedy*.

Stats show SubQ RFID chips increase the frequency of worker implants.

A closet filled with wedding dresses filed in ascending size.

Which towel should I use if the hypothetical mess I need to clean
       is blood?

The mind can be a couch or the space under it and still come up with
       the same thing.

Artificial intelligence is a framed doctorate diploma.

The angry woman has her own reasons as well as her mother's.

Beauty is a bunch of organized holes in the face.

I need to stop buying beer so I save enough money to do the things I want like buy beer.

Hang on a moment while I look at photos of this new spider.

Blowjobs are the Rome of everything after Rome.

Only desperate people actually believe they'll be better by Thursday.

I've lost track of what *favourite* even means.

Smooth jazz is God's peristaltic grumble.

What if we are flown like kites from a ground beyond the grave?

Restart the stop-time of this moment with trumpet blat and a James Brown scream.

Vice screws itself tight around your head.

The end happens when the poisons reach the children.

Wallpaper everything with Ebola maps.

How many times do I have to tell Paul Celan I'm sorry?

Joy lasts as long as distraction.

Listen to the background hum of the dishwasher.

What will happen when Santa figures out how to spread our sins among the whole family?

Everyone is one measure or another away from jackass.

This year I'm giving the gift of shutting the fuck up.

#GloryGloryHolelluja

Anything in Creation can be used as a hammer.

Set poetry down in a storm and watch it become the storm.

Every armchair a valiant steed put out to stud.

My son has started another Instagram account I will have to watch.

What happens in Vegans stays in Vegans.

The children first learn to ransom through tears.

Click every object with your eyes to ensure it's not concealing secret 1ups.

Killers are fairy tales not content to remain unread.

Wearing French cuffs says as much about you as ordering cassis.

Common household pests photobomb moments of microscopic bliss.

Age dampens your need to be always right.

Profile photos allow me to keep up on the narrow missus misses.

There is no traction in memory's mud puddle.

I'd have long since lost a hand to the wheelchair spokes.

What I'd give to once again be unable to distinguish between a
   human and a marionette.

Cash in your lifetime *likes* for poker chips.

There were the years spent wanting to comb Chewbacca and then this.

God and Disney continue to animate useful objects for fun.

Old folks are champions of moments in the process of being forgotten.

Childhood remains loveseats and ashtrays and a box of Black Magic.

Allot decent time in your schedule for blinking against the light.

Make verse as reliable and rooted as white headstones in
   a Pentecostal graveyard.

Electrics buzz and crackle like a derby girl's knees.

Young people act as though everything's been leading up to vaping.

Baguette gets slapped down on the counter like a show-off's knobbly cock.

Faith is knowing thought happens even by accident.

Why isn't it tsunami season yet?

I learned to talk just so I could say all this shit.

People mime screaming at other people from inside their cars.

Shame's underwear band folds below age's belly.

Everywhere you look some parents are killing their kids.

Don't dwarf planets sound like they'd have the most darling
     singing aliens?

A Hindu woman yelling at you is some seriously scary shit.

It's hard to tell whether the scooter or the weight problem came first.

Life is a process of trying to get your consumer data to match your
     best intentions.

Stats say no one is subscribing to our Lord's Prayer podcast.

Let me know when the phi phenomenon kicks in.

I am just trying to maintain integergrity in an increasingly irrational
     world.

Blow or bite or wait on the other side.

Punching holes in things is how all the best hammers pray.

The noblesse oblige part will happen when I point but say nothing.

#TheBookOfRevolutions

Be strong and discreet in how you end things.

Enter every room and immediately scout out the emergency exists.

Our tiny reflective robots sprinkle infections over planets we hope to one day shit on.

The most prevalent disability is thought/no thought (circle one).

It's increasingly difficult to not offer a direct assessment.

Lenticular clouds hover as though picking a spot to start their counterstrike.

Every point is terminal in infinity.

Paying dues to people more privileged than you is called *culture*.

You say *I love you* and I say *I love YouTube*.

Seek religiously battery LEDs not flashing red.

The huge bellies and dangly bits of naked old men look dredged from the sea.

Scientists chip away at our constants as effectively as priests shore them up.

No one ever talks about all the goats at the mountain's foot.

Warship is just a misspelling of *worship*.

Schrödinger's babies wriggle under the rubble.

How do you provide a buck and change in an age dedicated to penny nails?

Death continues to be a mostly boom industry.

I was baptized in utero by rum and Marlboros.

Set a circus-worth of zebras end on end and climb the stripes.

Teeth grind down in the face of performed politics.

Irony and parody fucked one night and left us this kid to raise.

You can raise up or you can raze down.

Direct all self-harm into one spot and hope it's not lethal.

If the world had a biography it would be titled *Are You Fucking Kidding Me?*

The difference between a six pack and a small keg is 15 years and a bad marriage.

My people are only recently mutted.

Who needs art when you got a hatred of women and a selfie of your dick?

The life coaches are tsking.

You now own all the blood I can spare for my enemies.

Photon sails unfold in space like God's hankies.

Fuel lights continue to blink their tyrant orders.

Consciousness is a virus infecting the brain's software.

I wish I didn't have an opinion on the root of our nastiness.

Please consider this slapping you as foreplay.

I made a deal with the Devil that I don't plan to honour.

How easy it would be if the choice was really only red pill or blue pill.

Death the crash and sleep the logout.

Negotiating the point at which I won't bear anymore is more exhausting than just bearing.

The emergency is there is no emergency.

Dozing will overtake me the moment I finish typing this line.

Is this thing even on?

Notes

Thanks to: Mark Callanan, Michael Holmes, David McGimpsey, Sina Queyras, Emily Schultz, Carmine Starnino.

Thanks to granting bodies: the Canada Council for the Arts, the Newfoundland Arts Council, and the City of St. John's.

Early excerpts were published in *Hazlitt* and *Lemon Hound*.

Thanks most of all to Elisabeth de Mariaffi.

Library and Archives Canada Cataloging in Publication

Murray, George, 1971–, author
    Diversion / written by George Murray.

ISBN: 978-1-77041-248-4 (PBK)
Also issued as: 978-1-77090-770-6 (EPUB);
978-1-77090-769-0 (PDF)

1. Title.
PS8576.U6814D58 2015   C811'.6   C2015-902778-0
c2015-902779-9

Editor for the press:
Michael Holmes/a misFit book
Cover design: David Gee
Typesetting: Lynn Gammie
Printing: Coach House 5 4 3 2 1

Purchase the print edition and receive the eBook free! For details, go to ecwpress.com/eBook.

MISFIT

Ontario
Ontario Media Development Corporation

ONTARIO ARTS COUNCIL
CONSEIL DES ARTS DE L'ONTARIO
an Ontario government agency
un organisme du gouvernement de l'Ontario

Canada Council
for the Arts

Conseil des Arts
du Canada

Canadä

The publication of *Diversion* has been generously supported by the Canada Council for the Arts which last year invested $157 million to bring the arts to Canadians throughout the country, and by the Ontario Arts Council (OAC), an agency of the Government of Ontario, which last year funded 1,793 individual artists and 1,076 organizations in 232 communities across Ontario, for a total of $52.1 million. We also acknowledge the financial support of the Government of Canada through the Canada Book Fund for our publishing activities, and the contribution of the Government of Ontario through the Ontario Book Publishing Tax Credit and the Ontario Media Development Corporation.